Writing Skills

Grade 1

Flash Kids

Spark Publishing

Illustrated by Clive Scruton

ISBN-13: 978-1-4114-0479-3
ISBN-10: 1-4114-0479-3

For more information, please visit *www.flashkidsbooks.com*
Please submit changes or report errors to *www.flashkidsbooks.com/errors*

Printed and bound in China

Spark Publishing
120 Fifth Avenue
New York, NY 10011

Dear Parent,

Reading and writing well are essential tools for success in all school subjects, at every grade level. In addition, many states now include writing assessments in their standardized tests, which are right around the corner for your first-grader. There may be no precise formula for good writing, but through studying and practicing sentences and paragraphs, your child will build the skills and versatility to approach any writing assignment with ease and confidence.

The six units in this fun, colorful workbook will guide your child from recognizing different kinds of words, to identifying and forming sentences, to putting events in sequence, to writing simple paragraphs and letters. Since your first-grader is still developing reading skills, you may wish to read the workbook pages aloud together. In answering the questions, your child will practice writing words and complete sentences on the ample writing lines. Check that he or she forms uppercase and lowercase letters correctly, and offer praise for good handwriting. Have crayons available, since many inspirational activities ask your first-grader to draw pictures that reflect his or her own sentences.

Here are some helpful suggestions for getting the most out of this workbook:

- Provide a quiet place to work.
- Go over the directions together.
- Encourage your child to do his or her best.
- Check each activity when it is complete.
- Review your child's work together, noting good work as well as points for improvement.

As your child completes the units, help him or her maintain a positive attitude about writing. Provide writing opportunities such as a notepad to keep shopping lists, and even a journal in which your child can write about things that happen each day and can keep a running list of ideas for paragraphs and letters. Continue to read to your child every day, and display his or her writing in your home.

Most importantly, enjoy this time you spend together. Your child's writing skills will improve even more with your dedication and support!

Proofreading Marks

Use the following symbols to help make proofreading faster.

MARK	MEANING	EXAMPLE
◯	spell correctly	Today is a ⟨specail⟩ day. *special*
⊙	add period	It is Kevin's birthday⊙
?	add question mark	Do you celebrate birthdays at school?
≡	use capital letter	My teacher's name is Mrs. baker.
℘	take out	She teaches us something new every every day.
¶	indent paragraph	¶ Yesterday, we learned how to sing a song about an octopus. First, she taught us the words. Then we sang it with a tune. Mrs. Baker even played her guitar as we sang.

Table of Contents

Unit 1: Words, Words, Words

HOW MUCH DO YOU KNOW?

Look at the words below. Circle the nouns. Draw a line under the verbs.

run ✓   desk   store   chair

chase ✓   coin   plane   jump ✓

bench   bird   car   swim ✓

girl   go ✓   walk ✓   skip ✓

What Is a Noun?

A noun names a person, a place, or a thing.

Look at the Word Bank. Circle the nouns in the box. Then write them on the lines. Color the picture.

WORD BANK

jump

clown

balloons

float

boy

dog

walk

boat

man

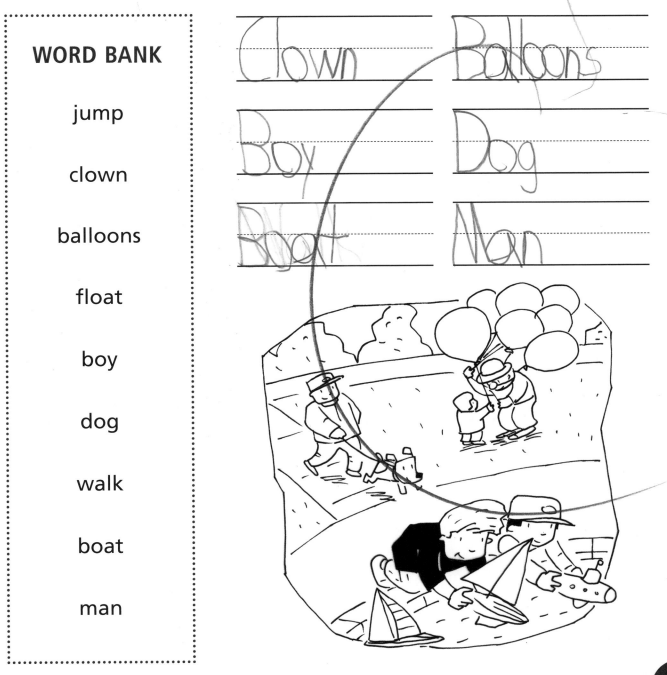

Clown   Balloons

Boy   Dog

Boat   Man

Picturing Nouns

Draw a picture of your classroom. On the lines below, write four nouns that are shown in your picture.

_____   _____

_____   _____

Exact Nouns

Good writers use exact nouns to make their writing better.

Read these sentences:

The animal runs.
The dog runs.

Both sentences tell that something runs.
The second sentence tells what kind of
animal runs. Dog is a more exact noun than animal. When you
use exact nouns, the reader will know what you really mean.

**Read each sentence below. Think of a more exact noun to replace
the underlined word. Then write the new word on the line.**

Dan likes to play sports. _____

I love to eat food. _____

My grandma bought me a new toy. _____

Mom cooks in the room. _____

What Is a Verb?

> A verb is a word that shows something happening.

Look at each picture. Circle the verb above it that describes what happens in each picture. Then write it on the line.

swim   climb   pool

_____

fall   run   shoes

_____

sleep   book   read

_____

hop   frog   legs

_____

My Superhero

Think up a new superhero. Draw a picture of the superhero in the box below. Then fill in the blanks below with verbs that describe what your superhero can do.

[drawing box]

_____   _____

My superhero can _____ , _____ ,

_____   _____

_____ , and _____ .

Exact Verbs

> Good writers use exact verbs to make their writing better.

Read these sentences:

"Come back!" she said.
"Come back!" she shouted.

Both sentences tell what the woman said. See how the second sentence tells how she said it. The word <u>shouted</u> is a more exact verb. When you write, use exact verbs so that the reader knows what you really mean.

Read each of the verbs below. Choose a word from the Verb Bank that is a more exact verb. Write the words on the line.

say _____

look _____

go _____

drink _____

VERB BANK

yell

skip

sip

peek

Adjectives

An adjective is a word that tells about, or describes, a noun.

Look at each picture. Draw a line under the adjective that describes the things in the picture. Then write the correct word.

sunny   girl   water   _____

angry   new   ride   _____

cry   careful   messy   _____

wet   old   build   _____

All Mixed Up

The word pairs below do not make sense. Circle the adjectives. On the lines below, write the adjectives next to the correct nouns.

soft dinner   salty weather   delicious hair

curly pillow   green popcorn   sunny grass

_____   _____

_____ dinner   _____ weather

_____   _____

_____ hair   _____ pillow

_____

_____ popcorn

_____

_____ grass

Feeling Words

Look at the faces below. Beneath each picture, write two words that describe how the person is feeling. Use words from the Word Bank.

WORD BANK

sad	happy	shocked	upset
angry	mad	surprised	glad

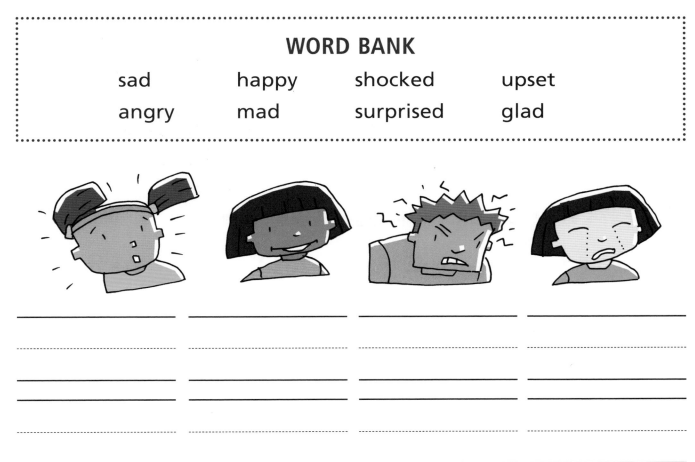

Draw a picture to show how you are feeling. Next to the picture, write a word that describes how you are feeling.

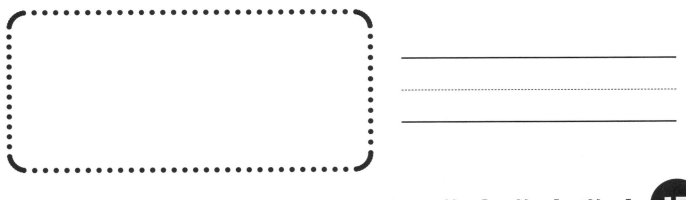

Pronouns

> A pronoun is a special word that can take the place of a noun.

Read these sentences:

Maria made a sandwich.
She made a sandwich.

The second sentence uses the word she. She is a pronoun. It takes the place of the word Maria.

These words are pronouns: I, he, she, it, we, you, they

Circle the pronoun in each of these sentences. Then write it on the line.

_____

Every morning, we ride the bus to school. _____

_____

It is very crowded. _____

_____

Peter asks, "Do you want to sit here?" _____

_____

Peter makes room for me. _____

Capital Letters for Names and Places

The names of people and places begin with a capital letter.

Look at the facts from the book report below. Then write the report using correct capital letters.

Grandma's House

Author: nathan thompson

Main characters:
grandma rose and billy

Setting: denton, texas

_____

Author: _____

Main characters: _____ and _____

Setting: _____ , _____

Titles for People

A title for a person begins with a capital letter
and usually ends with a period.

TITLES   Mr.   Mrs.   Miss   Ms.   Dr.

**Read each sentence. Circle the titles that are written incorrectly.
Then write the sentences correctly.**

1. mr Grayson is our bus driver.

_____

_____

2. I went to see dr Hubbard for a check-up.

_____

_____

3. My piano teacher is miss Marks.

_____

_____

4. mr and mrs Nelson live next door to us.

_____

_____

Days of the Week

The names of the days of the week begin with capital letters.

Find and circle the seven days of the week in the word search puzzle below. Look across and down. Then write your favorite day of the week on the line below.

```
k  f  h  m  v  b  n  W  p  c
s  S  u  n  d  a  y  e  i  F
d  c  e  d  f  x  o  d  d  r
p  d  a  c  S  u  g  n  a  i
M  o  n  d  a  y  j  e  y  d
i  g  r  u  t  d  i  s  u  a
r  f  T  h  u  r  s  d  a  y
h  a  u  w  r  v  t  a  y  m
b  y  e  n  d  d  c  y  l  j
c  o  s  y  a  a  o  k  c  t
x  m  d  f  y  y  d  a  y  s
n  s  a  b  u  m  e  t  s  b
w  s  y  x  s  k  p  r  l  k
```

_____

_____

_____

Special Days

The names of holidays and special days begin with capital letters.

Each holiday or special day needs capital letters. Even the word <u>day</u> should be capitalized when it is written after the name of the holiday.

Circle the holiday or special day in each sentence. Then write the words correctly in the blanks below.

Mom gave me a box of chocolates on valentine's day.

_____

_____

presidents' day is also in February.

_____

_____

I gave my mom a pretty dress for mother's day.

_____

_____

For memorial day, we had a picnic in the park.

_____

_____

Synonyms

> Synonyms (say: sin-OH-nims) are words that mean the same thing.

Good writers use synonyms to make their writing more interesting. The words below are synonyms for the word <u>big</u>. Read the meaning of each word.

big	of great size
loud	easy to hear, loud in volume
tall	not short
old	having many years

Read each sentence. Choose a better word to write in place of the word <u>big</u>. Then write the sentence with the new word.

My brother is not <u>big</u> enough to go to school yet.

_____

_____

We do not use <u>big</u> voices in the library.

_____

_____

Antonyms

Antonyms (say: ant-OH-nims) are words that mean the opposite of each other.

The words <u>up</u> and <u>down</u> are antonymns.

The balloon goes <u>up</u>.

The balloon comes <u>down</u>.

In each group, draw a line to match the word to its opposite, or antonymn.

open	on
off	sit
out	in
stand	cry
laugh	close

Make a List

Think of a person, a place, or a thing. Then make a list of words that describe it, but don't tell what it is. Give the list to a friend and see if he or she can tell you what the object is.

These are words that describe the person, place, or thing I am thinking of:

_____

_____

_____

_____

_____

_____

_____

_____

Review

Circle the words that are adjectives. Underline the words that are pronouns.

pretty	she	soft
you	I	nice
angry	happy	he
it	thin	sleepy
old	kind	brown
loud	they	we

Write a word that is a synonym for each word.

cold   _____

sleepy   _____

nice   _____

UNIT 2: What Is a Sentence?

HOW MUCH DO YOU KNOW?

In each pair, circle the group of words that is a sentence.

Alex does a cartwheel.

All over the playground

Singing at the top of her lungs

Mrs. Durand is my music teacher.

Look out!

Under the sofa

Write the following sentence correctly.

We had a lot of rain in april

_____

_____

_____

_____

Complete Sentences

> A sentence tells a complete thought or idea.

Read these sentences:

Matthew solved the puzzle.
Solved the puzzle

The first group of words is a sentence that tells a complete idea. It tells about something Matthew did. The second group of words does not tell who solved the puzzle. It is not a sentence.

Look at the pictures below. Draw a line to the sentence that tells about the picture.

   Rufus sleeps on the sofa.

   The flowers bloom.

   Beth paints a picture.

Which One Is a Sentence?

Some groups of words are not sentences. Circle the sentence in each pair and write it on the line below.

Our class takes a field trip.   Our class

_____

On a yellow school bus   We ride on a yellow school bus.

_____

Takes us to the zoo   The bus takes us to the zoo.

_____

We see all the animals.   All the animals

_____

Statements

A statement is a sentence that tells something. A statement begins with a capital letter and ends with a period. (.)

This is a statement:
I like to play soccer.

Circle the statement in each pair. Then write it correctly on the line below.

Our team has a game today.   Our team game

_____

_____

Out to the field   We go to the field.

_____

_____

The game begins.   When will the game begin?

_____

_____

Eddie kicks the ball.   Kicks the ball hard

_____

_____

Find the Statements

There are five statements in the box below. Underline the sentences that are statements. Write the five statements on the lines.

Dad is in the garage.

Able to leap

We have four tickets.

I can read a book.

Swimming in the lake

Do you like rabbits?

Bill has a pet goldfish.

I had a silly dream.

Commands

A command is a special kind of statement that tells someone to do something.

A command begins with a capital letter and ends with a period.

This is a command: Use soft voices in the library.

Circle the sentences below that are commands.

There are many books in the library.

What is your favorite book?

Choose a book.

Mrs. Masted is the librarian.

Take your book to the front desk.

Read silently to yourself.

Do you know where to sit?

Do not shout.

Find an empty chair and be seated.

How many pages have you read?

Questions

A question is a sentence that asks something.
A question begins with a capital letter and ends
with a question mark. (?)

Circle the question in each pair. Then write it correctly on the
line below.

Do you know the answer?   Knowing the answer

_____

What is it?   You can figure it out.

_____

From the chalkboard   Can you write it on the board?

_____

Checking your work.   Did you check your work?

_____

Find the Question

There are five questions in the box below. Underline the sentences that are questions. Write the five questions on the lines.

Did you hear that?   A soft, fluffy pillow?

Is anyone home?   Mom asked me a question.

Listening carefully   How do you feel?

What did you have for lunch?   Are you coming with us?

_____

- -

_____

- -

_____

- -

_____

- -

_____

- -

_____

Exclamations

An exclamation is a sentence that shows strong feeling. An exclamation begins with a capital letter and ends with an exclamation point. (!)

This is an exclamation: What a great shot!

Read the sentences below. Underline the sentences that are exclamations.

Look out!

Is that a monster?

You can have a banana.

That is fantastic news!

Wait for me!

Wake up!

I will not eat that!

I hate peanut butter!

When is your birthday?

Let's go home.

Capital Letters and End Marks

A sentence begins with a capital letter.
It ends with a period, an exclamation point,
or a question mark.

Circle the sentences below that are written correctly.

my family goes to the circus.

Have you ever been to the circus?

We sit in the fourth row

Dad gets us some popcorn.

we watch the clowns juggle

That is amazing!

Six lions jump through some hoops.

Can you believe they can do that.

How Does the Sentence End?

Rewrite the sentences and add the correct capital letters and end marks.

let's go to the carnival

_____

_____

do you want to ride the roller coaster

_____

_____

i will buy some cotton candy

_____

_____

can we play a game

_____

_____

you won a prize

_____

_____

Fix the Sentence

Look at each sentence carefully. Rewrite the sentence with correct capital letters and end marks.

mom comes in

_____

_____

she has a box

_____

_____

it is for us

_____

_____

what is it

_____

_____

it is a new toy

_____

_____

Sentence Subjects

The subject of a sentence names who or what the sentence is about. It is the naming part of the sentence.

Read this sentence:

The birds chirp in the nest.

This sentence is about the birds. <u>Birds</u> is the subject of this sentence.

Read the sentences below. Answer the questions to help you find the subject, or naming part, in each sentence. Write the subject on the line below.

Autumn is finally here. What is finally here?

_____

_____

The leaves are falling. What is falling?

_____

_____

Children bundle up in warmer clothes. Who bundles up?

_____

_____

Searching for Subjects

Read each sentence. Underline the subject, or naming part.

The skateboard is fast.

My dog ripped my homework.

We swim in the pool.

Dad and I go for a walk.

Katherine brushes her teeth.

Unit 2: What Is a Sentence?

Subject Match-Up

Complete each sentence with the correct subject, or naming part, from the Word Bank.

```
                        WORD BANK
     Yellow      baby      car      cake      Winter      radio
```

_____

The _____ tastes delicious.

_____

_____ is my favorite color.

_____

Your _____ is too loud!

_____

The _____ is crying.

_____

Our _____ is faster than his.

_____

_____ is my favorite season.

Sentence Predicates

The predicate of a sentence tells what the subject does, has, or is. It is the telling part of the sentence.

Read this sentence:
Jamie likes to fly her kite.

The subject of this sentence is <u>Jamie</u>. The sentence tells us that Jamie likes to fly her kite. The predicate of this sentence is <u>likes to fly her kite</u>.

Read each sentence. Underline the predicate, or telling part.

Our teacher is nice.

My breakfast tastes delicious.

Grandma and I bake cookies.

Queenie takes a nap.

Choose a Predicate

Look at the box of predicates, or telling parts. Choose a predicate to go with the subject in each sentence. Write the predicate on the line to complete the sentence.

smells lovely.

is friendly.

lives in a blue house.

is very short.

makes a lot of noise.

feels soft.

solved the puzzle.

growled at me.

Our neighbor _____

The flower _____

His pet dog _____

Word Order

Words in a sentence must be in an order that makes sense.

Rearrange each group of words and write the sentence correctly.

park. We to go the

_____

- -

_____

sits Grandma a on bench.

_____

- -

_____

the in Two ducks pond. swim

_____

- -

_____

Carlos ducks. the feeds

_____

- -

_____

water. splash They the in

_____

- -

_____

Sentence Switch

> The order of words can change the meaning of a sentence.

The two sentences below use the same words. See how the order of the words makes each sentence have a different meaning.

Lisa runs faster than Marcus.
Marcus runs faster than Lisa.

Rearrange the words to change the meaning of each sentence. Write the new sentence on the line below.

Mom called Grandma on the phone.

_____

_____

Erin is stronger than Peter.

_____

_____

The teacher borrowed a pencil from her student.

_____

_____

The dog chased the cat.

_____

_____

combining Sentences

Good writers combine sentences for better writing.

Read these sentences:
1. Mary likes fruit.
2. Mary likes vegetables.
3. Mary likes fruit and vegetables.

See how sentence 3 uses the word <u>and</u> to combine sentence 1 and sentence 2.

Read each pair of sentences.
Combine each pair into one sentence. Write it on the line below.

1. Rob can read.   Rob can write.

_____

_____

2. We ate pizza.   We ate hot dogs.

_____

_____

3. Chris plays basketball.   John plays basketball.

_____

_____

Complete the Sentences

Begin or finish each sentence. Use your imagination!
Remember to use correct capital letters and end marks.

_____

Emily likes to _____

_____

I wish I could _____

_____

_____ is the best movie I have

ever seen!

_____

I can't believe you _____

_____

_____ runs faster than my mom.

_____

The aliens told us to _____

Run-On Sentences

A run-on sentence is a sentence that has more than one idea or thought. Run-on sentences should be divided into two sentences.

This is a run-on sentence:
It is hot outside do you want to go swimming?

The run-on sentence has too many ideas. It should be divided into two sentences like this:
It is hot outside. Do you want to go swimming?

Read each run-on sentence. Then divide it into two sentences and write them correctly on the lines below.

The movie was cool it had a lot of car chases.

_____

_____

_____

_____

We ate popcorn it had a lot of butter on it.

_____

_____

_____

_____

Review

Write each sentence correctly on the line.

sam likes to play on the playground

_____

_____

do you want to go on the slide

_____

_____

mom pushes the swing i like to go very high

_____

_____

Read each sentence. Circle the subject. Draw a line under the predicate.

Emilio and Jana play tag.

The dog runs after them.

We like to play at the park.

UNIT 3: Sentence about a Picture

HOW MUCH DO YOU KNOW?

Look at each picture. Circle the group of words next to the picture that is a complete sentence.

We bake cookies.
baking cookies

throws the ball to me
He throws the ball.

Finish the sentence with the more exact word below it.

_____

Keisha gives her _____ a bath.

(dog, animal)

Studying a Sentence

A sentence tells a complete thought.
It begins with a capital letter and ends with an end mark.

Look at each picture. Circle the group of words below the picture that is a complete sentence.

Dad rakes the leaves.
falling on the ground

six years old
Today is my birthday.

lives in a bowl
I have a pet fish.

a pretty necklace
That is very pretty.

Sentence Matching

Look at each picture. Draw a line from the picture to the sentence that tells about the picture.

Jana hurt her knee.

The bug crawls on the leaf.

This tastes delicious!

Using Exact Words

Good writers use exact words to make their writing better.

Finish each sentence by choosing and writing the more exact word below it.

Tim gets a shiny, new _____ .

(bike, vehicle)

He _____ down the street.

(goes, rides)

He stops at the _____ .

(building, store)

Tim gives the clerk two _____ .

(quarters, coins)

Adding Adjectives

> Adjectives are describing words that make sentences more interesting.

Read these sentences:

The rabbit hopped behind the bush.

The white rabbit hopped behind the prickly bush.

The second sentence is more interesting because it has the adjectives <u>white</u> and <u>prickly</u>. <u>White</u> describes what the rabbit looks like. <u>Prickly</u> describes what the bush feels like.

Read each sentence. Add adjectives, or describing words, to each sentence. Write the new sentence on the line. You can use the words in the Word Bank to help you.

WORD BANK

cherry	sunny	colorful	silly	delicious
fresh	tasty	sandy	funny	

Mom made a pie.

_____

_____

We watched the clown do tricks.

_____

_____

Proofreading Sentences

PROOFREADING HINTS
- Be sure your sentence begins with a capital letter.
- Be sure your sentence ends with an end mark.

Read each sentence. Use the Proofreading Marks to correct the mistake in each sentence. Then write the sentence correctly. See the chart on page 4 to learn how to use the marks.

PROOFREADING MARKS	
⬭	spell correctly
⊙	add period
?	add question mark
≡	capitalize
ℒ	take out
¶	indent paragraph

most dogs are friendly animals.

_____

_____

They make good pets

_____

_____

Choose the Sentence

Look at each picture. Choose a sentence from the box that tells about it. Then write the sentence beneath the picture.

> The soup is too hot. In the woods My shoes are new.
>
> brand new shoes Camping is fun. alphabet soup
>
> We wash our car. soap and water running faster

_____

- - - - - - - - - - - - - -

_____

_____

- - - - - - - - - - - - - -

_____

Tell about the Pictures

Look at the pictures. Write a sentence to tell about each picture.

Over the Rainbow

Finish the picture. Then write a sentence about the picture.

_____

_____

_____

Up, Up, and Away

Finish the picture. Then write a sentence to tell about the picture.

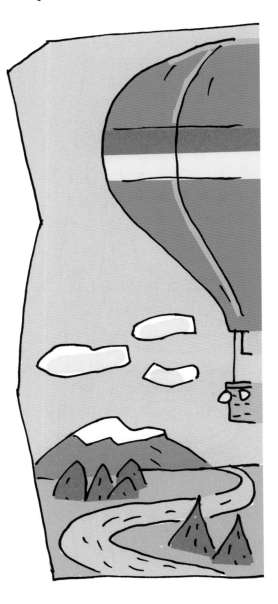

Family Dinner

Draw food on the table to finish the picture. Then write a sentence to tell about the picture.

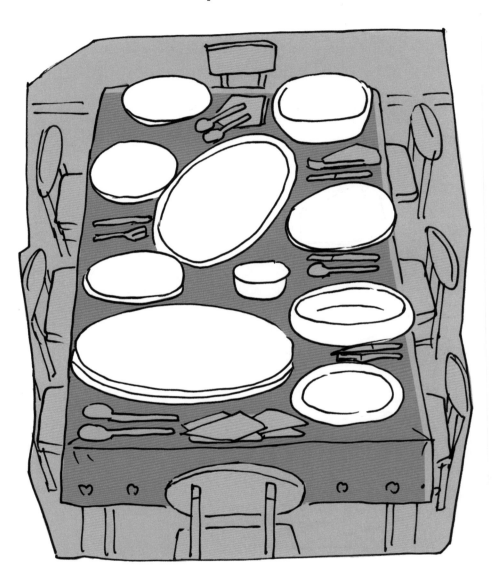

The Best Day Ever

Imagine that you could do anything you want today. Draw a picture to show what you would do. Write a sentence to tell about your picture.

Favorite Sport

Draw a picture that shows your favorite sport. Write a sentence to tell about your picture.

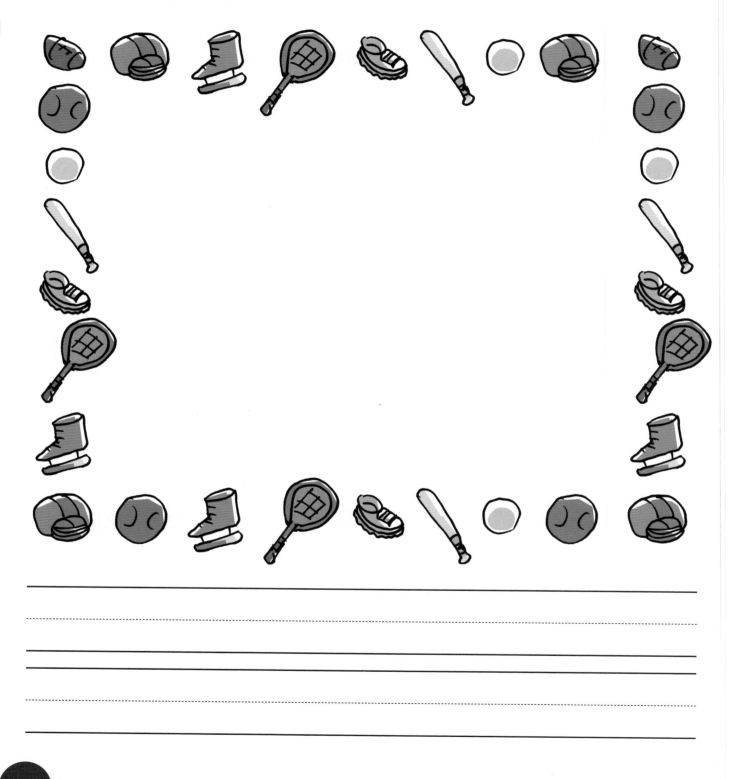

Pet Monster

Imagine that you have a pet monster. Draw a picture of your monster. Write a sentence to tell about your picture.

Favorite Subject

Which subject do you like best in school? Draw a picture to show your favorite subject. Write a sentence to tell about your picture.

My Bedroom

Draw a picture of your bedroom. Write a sentence to tell about your picture.

My Family

Draw a picture of your family. Write a sentence to tell about your picture.

Review

Look at the picture. Circle the sentence that tells about the picture.

Holding up traffic

The workers fix the road.

Wearing hard hats

Write another sentence that tells about the picture.

_____

. . . .

_____

UNIT 4: Writing and Completing Sentences

HOW MUCH DO YOU KNOW?

Think about things you like and things you do not like. Finish the sentences below. Be sure to end each sentence with an end mark.

My name is _____

I like _____

I do not like _____

Write a new sentence to tell something else about yourself. Remember to begin your sentence with a capital letter.

_____

_____

_____

Alphabet Sentence

Choose a letter of the alphabet. Draw a picture of something that begins with that letter. Then complete the sentence to tell about the picture.

_____ is for _____
(letter)

Colorful Sentences

Read the names of the color words below. Write a sentence to name something that comes in each color. The first one is done for you.

The sky is blue.

Having a Pet

Think about a pet you have or would like to have. Draw a picture of the pet. Then write complete sentences to answer the questions about your pet.

What kind of pet is it? _____

What is the name of your pet? _____

What does your pet eat? _____

Where does your pet sleep? _____

What does your pet like to do? _____

Sentences that Describe

Good writers use their five senses to make their sentences more interesting.

Draw a picture of your favorite food. Complete each sentence to describe the food.

_____

My favorite food is _____

It looks _____

When I pick it up, it feels _____

It smells _____

When I eat it, it sounds like _____

It tastes _____

Make a Wish

Imagine that you could have three wishes. What would you wish for? Complete the three sentences below and draw a picture of your favorite wish.

_____

First, I would wish _____

_____

Then, I would wish _____

_____

Last, I would wish _____

When I Grow Up...

Think about a job you would like to do when you grow up. Draw a picture of yourself doing the job. Complete the sentences below to tell about the job.

When I grow up, I would like to be a
_____
- -
_____

I want to have this job because
_____
- -
_____

The best part about this job would be
_____
- -
_____

Joke of the Day

Read this riddle. Tell why it is funny.

Question: Why are all numbers afraid of seven?
Answer: Because seven eight nine!

The riddle is funny because

_____

- -

_____

Do you know a funny joke or riddle? Write it on the lines below.

This is my joke!

_____

- -

_____

_____

- -

_____

_____

- -

_____

What I Like about You

Think about one of your friends. Then complete the sentences to tell good things about your friend.

My friend's name is
_____
....
_____

My friend is great because
_____
....
_____

My friend also
_____
....
_____

The best thing about my friend is
_____
....
_____

Be sure to tell your friend the nice things you wrote about him or her!

Once upon A Time

Think about your favorite fairy tale. Write sentences to answer the questions below.

What is the title of the fairy tale?

_____

_____

Who are the main characters?

_____

_____

What is the problem in the story?

_____

_____

How is the problem solved?

_____

_____

In My Dream

> Good writers write about events in order.

Think about a dream you had. Write a sentence to tell what happened first, next, and last.

In my dream, first

_____

_____

_____

_____

Next,

_____

_____

_____

_____

_____

Last,

_____

_____

_____

_____

_____

What Do You Do Best?

Think about something you do well. Then write sentences to answer the questions below. Be sure to start each sentence with a capital letter and end it with an end mark.

What is something you can do well?

_____

_____

How did you learn to do it well?

_____

_____

How long have you done it?

_____

_____

Who helped you learn to do it?

_____

_____

Comparisons

A comparison is a sentence that compares one thing to another. Good writers use comparisons to paint a better picture for the reader.

This is a comparison:
The kitten is as soft as a pillow.

Complete the comparisons below.

The librarian is as quiet as

_____

_____

The runner is faster than

_____

_____

The children on the playground are as wild as

_____

_____

My grandma is sweeter than

_____

_____

How Do You Feel?

Complete each sentence below to tell about a time when you felt a certain way. Remember to use an end mark at the end of each sentence.

I felt happy when
_____
....
_____

I felt scared when
_____
....
_____

I felt surprised when
_____
....
_____

I felt angry when
_____
....
_____

I felt embarrassed when
_____
....
_____

Weather Report

Draw a picture to show what the weather is like where you are today. Then write a sentence to describe the weather. Try to use as many adjectives, or describing words, as you can.

_____

_____

_____

_____

Far, Far Away

Think about a place you would like to travel. Complete the
sentences below.

I would like to go to

_____

. . . .

_____

When I got there, first I would

_____

. . . .

_____

Then, I would

_____

. . . .

_____

I would see

_____

. . . .

_____

In an Emergency

Imagine that you had an emergency. Think about what you would do to get help. Write what you would do first, next, and last.

First, I would

_____

_____

_____

Next, I would

_____

_____

_____

Last, I would

_____

_____

_____

Safety First

Think about some rules for bike safety. Write three sentences to tell three things a person can do to stay safe on a bicycle.

RULES FOR BIKE SAFETY

1. _____

2. _____

3. _____

My Favorite Story

Think about a story you have read. Write a sentence to answer each question below. Be sure to begin each sentence with a capital letter and end with an end mark.

What is the title of the story?

_____

_____

Who are the main characters?

_____

_____

Where did the story take place?

_____

_____

What happened at the beginning of the story?

_____

_____

How did the story end?

_____

_____

A Million Dollars

Imagine that you won a million dollars. What would you do with the money? Think about what you would do first, next, and last. Then complete each sentence below.

If I won a million dollars, first I would

_____

_____

Next, I would

_____

_____

Last, I would

_____

_____

My Favorite Season

Think about your favorite season. Then complete each sentence below.

My favorite season is

During this season, I wear

My favorite thing to do during this season is

Review

Read the questions below. Write a sentence to answer each question. Be sure to begin each sentence with a capital letter and end it with an end mark.

All About Me

What is your name?

_____

- -

_____

How old are you?

_____

- -

_____

What do you look like?

_____

- -

_____

What is the thing you like most about yourself?

_____

- -

_____

UNIT 5: Writing a Paragraph

HOW MUCH DO YOU KNOW?

Read the paragraph. Then answer the questions.

I love to visit the zoo. First, I go to the gorilla forest to watch gorillas play. Then, I go to see the giraffes. One eats leaves from a tall tree. Next, I visit the reptile house. Finally, I go to see the bird show.

What is the topic sentence?

_____

_____

What happens last in the story?

_____

_____

What Is the Topic?

A paragraph is a group of sentences that tells about one topic.

A paragraph has at least three sentences. The first sentence is indented. It begins a little to the right.

Good writers use details that tell only about the topic.

Read the story. Write the sentence that tells what the topic is. Underline the details that tell about the topic.

My room is a mess. There are clothes all over the floor. My bed is not made. My toys are scattered all over the room. It is so messy that I cannot walk across the room without hopping over piles of stuff.

What is the topic sentence?

_____

_____

_____

Reading a Personal Story

A personal story tells something you have done.
It can tell how you feel about something.
A story tells what happened in order.

Read the story.

    I love summer vacation! The best part is the camping trip I take with my family each year. We drive for three hours to the lake. We stay in a tent and swim in the lake. Every morning, my dad cooks scrambled eggs for breakfast.

Write a sentence that tells what you like to do during summer vacation.

_____

_____

_____

_____

Proofreading a Personal Story

> **PROOFREADING HINTS**
> - Be sure that the word <u>I</u> is a capital letter.
> - Be sure that each sentence begins with a capital letter.
> - Be sure that each sentence ends with an end mark.

Read the story. Use the Proofreading Marks to correct six mistakes.

PROOFREADING MARKS	
◯	spell correctly
⊙	add period
?	add question mark
≡	capitalize
℘	take out
¶	indent paragraph

one day, my brother and I went to an amusement park. First, we rode the carousel. Then, we raced to the go-karts. my brother almost crashed around around the last curve. Next, we waited in line for the roller coaster I was scared, but my brother told me it would be fun. He was rite. I had so much fun that we rode it again and again. i can't wait to go back to the amusement park!

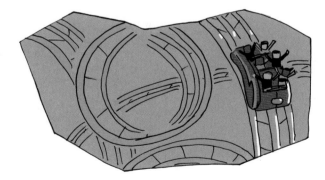

Saturday Afternoon

Think about what you did last Saturday afternoon. What happened first, next, and last? Write a paragraph about it.

_____

_____

_____

_____

_____

_____

_____

_____

_____

_____

When I Felt Sad

Write about a time when you were sad. What happened? Why did you feel sad? How did you feel better?

_____

- -
_____

- -
_____

- -
_____

- -
_____

- -
_____

My Favorite Restaurant

Imagine that you are visiting your favorite restaurant. What do you do first, next, and last? Write a paragraph about your visit.

_____

_____

_____

_____

_____

_____

_____

_____

_____

_____

_____

_____

_____

Reading a Paragraph that Describes

> A paragraph that describes tells what someone
> or something is like.
> The topic sentence names the topic.
> The other sentences give details about the topic.

Read the paragraph. Then answer the questions below.

My cat looks so sweet when she is sleeping. She makes a quiet purring sound. Her little chest moves up and down as she breathes. Her soft tail curls  around and brushes against her paw. Her eyes are closed tight. She has a gentle smile on her face.

What is the topic of the paragraph?

_____

....

_____

What are two detail sentences in the paragraph that tell about the topic?

_____

....

_____

....

_____

Proofreading a Paragraph that Describes

PROOFREADING HINTS
- Be sure to indent your paragraph.
- Be sure each sentence begins with a capital letter.
- Check your spelling.

PROOFREADING MARKS

◯	spell correctly
⊙	add period
?	add question mark
≡	capitalize
✨	take out
¶	indent paragraph

Read the paragraph. Use the Proofreading Marks to correct five mistakes.

What a wonderful day at the beach! The sun is shining down on the water. Lifeguards stand at the edge of the shore. children laugh and splash in the waves. A father bilds a sand castle with his son. I bury my toes deap in the warm sand and read a book

Delicious Dessert

Write a paragraph to describe your favorite dessert. Use adjectives to tell about the colors, the smells, and the flavors.

_____

_____

_____

_____

_____

_____

_____

_____

On the Playground

Imagine that you are playing on a playground. Write a paragraph to describe what you see, hear, feel, and smell.

_____

_____

_____

_____

_____

_____

_____

_____

_____

_____

_____

Story Order

Good writers write sentences in an order that makes sense.

Read the sentences. Write a number (1, 2, 3, 4, and 5) next to each sentence to put them in the correct order.

_____ A noise woke her up.

_____ Amelia turned on a light at the bottom of the stairs.

_____ She got out of bed and went downstairs.

_____ Amelia was sound asleep.

_____ She saw that her cat had knocked over a plant.

Writing in Story Order

Read the sentences. Write the sentences in order so that the story makes sense. Remember to indent the first sentence of the paragraph.

Then, we grab our towels and goggles.

Today we get to go swimming.

Finally, we go to the pool to swim.

First, we put on our swimsuits.

_____

- -

_____

_____

- -

_____

_____

- -

_____

_____

- -

_____

Write about the Planet X

Write a story about aliens on the imaginary planet called X.
Who lives on the planet? What do they do? What happens first,
second, and last?

Reading a Story

A story has a beginning, a middle, and an ending.
A story is often about solving a problem.
A story has a title.
It sometimes has more than one paragraph.

Read the story. Then answer the questions on the next page.

The Hiding Place

Julio loved playing hide-and-seek with the other children on his block. They were happy to let him play, but Julio was the youngest of the kids. No matter where he hid, Julio was always discovered by the older kids. They knew all the hiding places.

Today, Julio decided that he would have to find a hiding place that no one knew about. He searched and searched. Finally, he saw the tall bushes right next to Mr. Adam's house. Mr. Adam was not the friendliest neighbor, so Julio knew that the other kids would not want to hide or look near his house.

Quickly, Julio ran over to the bushes and sat behind them. He looked through the branches. One by one, the other kids ran and chased each other. At last, Julio was the only player left. When they finally called his name to come out, Julio stood up with a smile. He had finally won!

Reading a Story

Answer the questions about the story "The Hiding Place."

What is the title?

_____

_____

Who are the characters?

_____

_____

What is the problem?

_____

_____

How is the problem solved?

_____

_____

Adventure in the Woods

Answer the questions below to help you write a story about an adventure in the woods. Then write the story on the next page.

Who are the characters?

_____

- -

_____

Where does the story take place?

_____

- -

_____

What are the events in the story?

_____

- -

_____

What is the problem?

_____

- -

_____

How is the problem solved?

_____

- -

_____

Adventure in the Woods

Write a story about an adventure in the woods. Use the questions on page 104 to help you write.

_____

_____

_____

_____

_____

_____

_____

_____

_____

_____

_____

_____

(Continue on your own paper.)

New Kid in School

Write a story about a student who is new to your school. Before you write, think about who the characters will be. Think about the beginning, middle, and end to your story.

_____

_____

_____

_____

_____

_____

_____

_____

_____

_____

_____

_____

_____

_____

_____

_____

_____

_____

_____

(Continue on your own paper.)

Studying Directions

Read the directions carefully. Then read what Steven did.

Mrs. Graham told her students to follow these directions:

1. Take out a piece of construction paper.

2. Fold the paper in half to make a card.

3. Use a marker to decorate the outside of the card.

4. Use a pencil to write a message on the inside of the card.

Steven took out a piece of construction paper. He folded the paper in half to make a card. He wrote a message on the inside of the card with his pencil.

Write the direction that Steven forgot to follow.

_____

_____

_____

_____

Extra Information

When writing directions, good writers tell only about the topic. They do not give extra information.

Read the directions for washing a dog. Circle the sentence that does not belong in the directions.

How to Wash Your Dog

1. Fill the bathtub or washtub with water.

2. Add soap to the water.

3. Help your dog get into the tub.

4. Dogs are the best kind of pet.

5. Wash the dog's fur, but be careful not to get soap in your dog's eyes.

6. Dry your dog off with a towel.

How to Get Dressed

Think about how you get dressed in the morning. What do you do first, second, and last? Write directions for how to get dressed below.

_____

....

1. _____

_____

....

2. _____

_____

....

3. _____

_____

....

4. _____

Writing Directions

HOW DO YOU DO THAT?

Think about something you know how to do. Write step-by-step directions below.

_____

HOW TO _____

_____

1. _____

_____

2. _____

_____

3. _____

_____

4. _____

Review

Read the paragraph. Write the sentences in an order that makes sense. Be sure to begin each sentence with a capital letter and end each sentence with an end mark.

After he got dressed, he ate breakfast. Then, he put on his clothes. Miguel had to get ready for school. Finally, he brushed his teeth. First, he got out of bed.

_____

_____

_____

_____

_____

_____

_____

UNIT 6: Writing a Letter

HOW MUCH DO YOU KNOW?

Read the letter. Use red to circle the greeting. Use blue to circle the signature. Use green to circle the closing.

Then answer the question about the letter.

March 3, 2005

Dear Grandma,
   I'm so glad that you came to visit last week. It was fun to show you my classroom. I'm also glad you got to meet my teacher, Mrs. Smith. I will miss having breakfast with you in the morning. I am looking forward to seeing you again this summer!

Love,
Yolanda

On what date was the letter written?

_____

_____

Parts of a Letter

A friendly letter has five parts. They are the heading, greeting, body, closing, and signature.

Look at the letter below and read the labels for each part. Then answer the questions below.

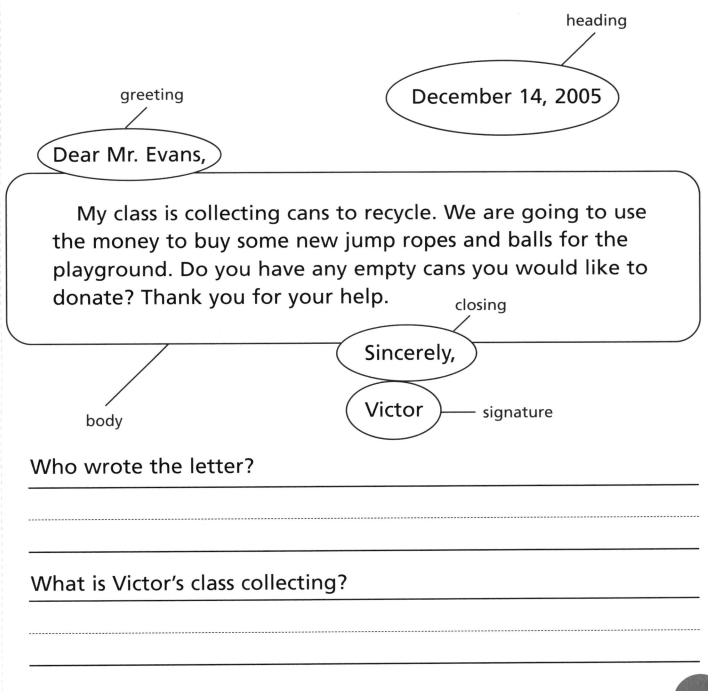

heading

December 14, 2005

greeting

Dear Mr. Evans,

My class is collecting cans to recycle. We are going to use the money to buy some new jump ropes and balls for the playground. Do you have any empty cans you would like to donate? Thank you for your help.

closing

Sincerely,

Victor — signature

body

Who wrote the letter?

_____

_____

What is Victor's class collecting?

_____

_____

Label the Letter Parts

Read the letter. Circle each part of the letter. Use different colors.

Circle the heading with red.

Circle the closing with yellow.

Circle the greeting with blue.

Circle the signature with orange.

Circle the body with green.

> June 2, 2005
>
> Dear Mrs. Simms,
>   Thank you for being my teacher this year. You helped me learn so much. I loved learning the songs you taught us. My favorite song was the one about the speckled frogs. I will miss you next year. Have a great summer vacation!
>
>   Your student,
>   Kelly

Addressing an Envelope

A letter is sent in an envelope. The center of the envelope has the address of the person who is receiving the letter. The top left corner has the address for the person who is sending the letter.

This is an envelope that Mark Smith sent to Juan Alvarez:

Mark Smith
923 Maple Drive
Evanston, Illinois 60201

Juan Alvarez
5423 Riggs Way
Houston, Texas 77077

Pretend you are addressing a letter to your teacher. Write the name of your teacher and the school address. Then write your own name and your home address in the top left corner.

Reading a Friendly Letter

Read the letter. Then answer the questions below.

July 8, 2005

Dear Mom and Dad,

   Camp is a lot of fun. I am making lots of friends. Today, we went horseback riding. We followed a trail down to the lake. Then we got off the horses and went for a swim. After dinner, we sat by a campfire and sang songs. I will teach them to you when I get home! I hope you are doing well.

Your son,
Jamal

Who wrote the letter?

_____

_____

To whom did he write the letter?

_____

_____

What did he do after dinner?

_____

_____

Proofreading a Friendly Letter

PROOFREADING HINTS
- Be sure that the first sentence of the body is indented.
- Be sure that each sentence ends with an end mark.
- Check your spelling.

Read the letter. Use the Proofreading Marks to correct five mistakes.

September 12, 2005

Dear ashley,
I hope you like your new house. I was very sad to see you move away, but I know you will make lots of friends at your new school. My mom says that we can visit soon I can't wait! I will bring your favorite game. We can eat pizza and stay up all night, just like we used to do. I mis you very much. Please write write back soon!

Your friend,
Vonda

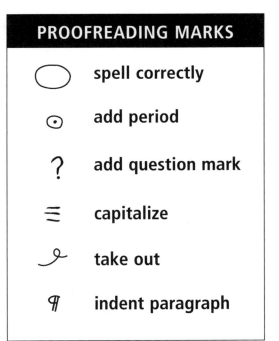

PROOFREADING MARKS	
◯	spell correctly
⊙	add period
?	add question mark
≡	capitalize
ℒ	take out
¶	indent paragraph

Writing a Friendly Letter

Pretend that you are on a vacation. Write a friendly letter to a friend. Tell your friend where you are and what you are doing. Remember to include all five parts of a letter.

Reading a Thank-You Letter

Read the letter. Then answer the questions below.

> January 30, 2005
>
> Dear Officer Brown,
>   Thank you so much for coming to our class. It was really nice of you to talk to us about bike safety. We learned a lot. When I got home, I checked my helmet to make sure it was the right size. It was too small. My dad is going to get me a new helmet today after school. I will wear it every day. I will also remember to look both ways before I cross the street.
>
> Sincerely,
> Robert Chavez

To whom did Robert write the letter?
_____
....
_____

What did Officer Brown talk to Robert's class about?
_____
....
_____

Who is going to buy Robert a new helmet?
_____
....
_____

Proofreading a Thank-You Letter

PROOFREADING HINTS
- Be sure to use capital letters to begin names and months.
- Check your spelling.

Read the letter. Use the Proofreading Marks to correct six mistakes.

PROOFREADING MARKS

◯	spell correctly
⊙	add period
?	add question mark
≡	capitalize
℘	take out
¶	indent paragraph

november 12, 2005

Dear Aunt Rebecca,

   Thnak you so much for the pretty scarf it was such a nice birthday gift. Now that the weather is getting cooler here, I think I will wear it almost every day! each time I wear it, I will think of you and smile.

   Love,

   haley

Writing a Thank-You Letter

Imagine that a family relative, such as an uncle, gave you a nice birthday gift. Write a thank-you letter for the gift. Be sure to tell your relative what you like most about the gift. Remember to include all five parts of a letter.

Reading an Invitation

AN INVITATION INCLUDES
- the name of the person you are inviting
- what the person is invited to
- the date, time, and place of the event
- your name

Read this invitation. Then answer the questions below.

March 12, 2005

Dear Sarah,

Please come to our school carnival. It will be held on March 26 from 9:00 a.m. until 4:00 p.m. at Rummel Creek Elementary School. There will be lots of rides and games. I hope you can come!

Your friend,
Omar

Who is invited?

_____

_____

What is the person invited to attend?

_____

_____

Writing an Invitation

Read the information below. Use the information to write an invitation to a friend.

> What is it? A surprise party for Meghan
>
> Date: February 2, 2006
>
> Time: 4:00 p.m.
>
> Place: Rollerworld Skating Rink

Make Your Own Invitation

Pretend you are having a party. Write an invitation to your friend. Remember to include the date, time, and place of the party.

Please come to
my party!

Review

Read the letter. Then answer the questions.

March 14, 2005

Dear Mr. Smith,

    I'm sorry that I dented your car door. I was learning to ride my new bike and I did not stop fast enough. I accidentally hit the door with the front wheel of my bike. I am saving money every week, and I would like to pay to fix the dent. Please tell me how much it will cost.

Sincerely,
Jake

Who wrote the letter?

_____

_____

Why did this person write the letter?

_____

_____

_____

Answer Key

Unit 1: Words, Words, Words

p. 6

Circle: desk, store, chair, coin, plane, bench, bird, car, girl.

Underline: run, chase, jump, swim, go, walk, skip

p. 7

Circle and write: clown, balloons, boy, dog, boat, and man

p. 8

any four nouns that can be found in a classroom

p. 9

Answers will vary, but should be exact nouns.

p. 10

swim

run

read

hop

p. 11

Answers will vary, but should be action verbs.

p. 12

yell

peek

skip

sip

p. 13

sunny

new

messy

wet

p. 14

delicious dinner

sunny weather

curly hair

soft pillow

salty popcorn

green grass

p. 15

shocked, surprised

happy, glad

angry, mad

sad, upset

p. 16

we

it

you

Me

p. 17

Nathan Thompson

Grandma Rose and Billy

Denton, Texas

p. 18

Mr. Grayson is our bus driver.

I went to see Dr. Hubbard for a check-up.

My piano teacher is Miss Marks.

Mr. and Mrs. Nelson live next door to us.

p. 19

k	f	h	m	v	b	n	W	p	c
s	S	u	n	d	a	y	e	i	F
d	c	e	d	f	x	o	d	d	r
p	d	a	c	S	u	g	n	a	i
M	o	n	d	a	y	j	e	y	d
i	g	r	u	t	d	i	s	u	a
r	f	T	h	u	r	s	d	a	y
h	a	u	w	r	v	t	a	y	m
b	y	e	n	d	d	c	y	l	j
c	o	s	y	a	a	o	k	c	t
x	m	d	f	y	y	d	a	y	s
n	s	a	b	u	m	e	t	s	b
w	s	y	x	s	k	p	r	l	k

Possible answers:

Sunday

Monday

Tuesday

Wednesday

Thursday

Friday

Saturday

p. 20

Valentine's Day

Presidents' Day

Mother's Day

Memorial Day

p. 21

My brother is not old enough to go to school yet.

We do not use loud voices in the library.

p. 22

open, close

off, on

out, in

stand, sit

laugh, cry

p. 24

Circle: pretty, soft, nice, angry, happy, thin, sleepy, old, kind, brown, loud.

Underline: she, you, I, he, it, they, we.

Answers to synonyms will vary.

Unit 2: What Is a Sentence?

p. 25

Alex does a cartwheel.

Mrs. Durand is my music teacher.

Look out!

We had a lot of rain in April.

p. 26

Picture 1: The flowers bloom.

Picture 2: Rufus sleeps on the sofa.

Picture 3: Beth paints a picture.

p. 27

Our class takes a field trip.

We ride on a yellow school bus.

The bus takes us to the zoo.

We see all the animals.

p. 28

Our team has a game today.

We go to the field.

The game begins.

Eddie kicks the ball.

p. 29

Underline and write: Dad is in the garage. We have four tickets. I can read a book. Bill has a pet goldfish. I had a silly dream.

p. 30

Circle: Choose a book. Take your book to the front desk. Read silently to yourself. Do not shout. Find an empty chair and be seated.

p. 31

Do you know the answer?

What is it?

Can you write it on the board?

Did you check your work?

p. 32

Underline and write: Did you hear that? Is anyone home? How do you feel? What did you have for lunch? Are you coming with us?

p. 33

Underline: Look out! Wake up! I will not eat that! I hate peanut butter! That is fantastic news! Wait for me!

p. 34

Circle:

Have you ever been to the circus?

Dad gets us some popcorn.

That is amazing!

Six lions jump through some hoops.

p. 35

Let's go to the carnival.

Do you want to ride the roller coaster?

I will buy some cotton candy.

Can we play a game?

You won a prize!

p. 36

Mom comes in.

She has a box.

It is for us.

What is it?

It is a new toy.

p. 37

Autumn

The leaves

Children

p. 38

The skateboard

My dog

We

Dad and I

Katherine

p. 39

cake

Yellow

radio

baby

car

Winter

p. 40

is nice

tastes delicious

bake cookies

takes a nap

p. 42

We go to the park.

Grandma sits on a bench.

Two ducks swim in the pond.

Carlos feeds the ducks.

They splash in the water.

p. 43

Grandma called Mom on the phone.

Peter is stronger than Erin. The student

borrowed a pencil from her teacher.

The cat chased the dog.

p. 44

Rob can read and write.

We ate pizza and hot dogs.

Chris and John play basketball.

p. 46

The movie was cool. It had a lot of car chases.

We ate popcorn. It had a lot of butter on it.

p. 47

Sam likes to play on the playground.

Do you want to go on the slide?

Mom pushes the swing.

I like to go very high.

Circled: Emilio and Jana

Underlined: play tag

Circled: The dog

Underlined: runs after them

Circled: We

Underlined: like to play at the park

Unit 3: Sentence about a Picture

p. 48

We bake cookies.

He throws the ball.

Keisha gives her dog a bath.

p. 49

Dad rakes the leaves.

Today is my birthday.

I have a pet fish.

That is very pretty.

p. 50

Picture 1: This tastes delicious!

Picture 2: Jana hurt her knee.

Picture 3: The bug crawls on the leaf.

p. 51

bike

rides

store

quarters

p. 53

most dogs are friendly animals.

They make good pets

p. 54

This soup is too hot.

We wash our car.

My shoes are new.

Camping is fun.

p. 65

Circle: The workers fix the road.

Unit 4: Writing and Completing Sentences

p. 83

Answers will vary, but might include: Wear a helmet. Look both ways before crossing a street. Stay on the sidewalk. Use hand signals.

p. 86

Answers will vary, but should include descriptions appropriate to the season.

Unit 5: Writing a Paragraph

p. 88

I love to visit the zoo.

The writer goes to see the bird show.

p. 89

Topic: My room is a mess.

Underlining may vary, but your child may have underlined clothes all over the floor, bed is not made, toys are scattered, cannot walk, piles of stuff

p. 91

one day, my brother and I went to an amusement park. First, we rode the carousel. Then, we raced to the go-karts. my brother almost crashed around around the last curve. Next, we waited in line for the roller coaster I was scared, but my brother told me it would be fun. He was rite. I had so much fun that we rode it again and again. i can't wait to go back to the amusement park!

p. 95

My cat looks so sweet when she is sleeping. Answers will vary but may include any of the last five sentences of the paragraph.

p. 96

What a wonderful day at the beach! The sun is shining down on the water. Lifeguards stand at the edge of the shore. children laugh and splash in the waves. A father bilds a sand castle with his son. I bury my toes deap in the warm sand and read a book

p. 99

2, 4, 3, 1, 5

p. 100

Today we get to go swimming. First, we put on our swimsuits. Then, we grab our towels and goggles. Finally, we go to the pool to swim.

p. 103

The Hiding Place
Julio and other children
Julio did not have a good hiding place.
Julio hid behind the tall bushes beside Mr. Adam's house.

p. 107

The direction Steven did not follow is: Use a marker to decorate the outside of the card.

p. 108

Circle: 4. Dogs are the best kind of pet.

p. 111

Miguel had to get ready for school. First, he got out of bed. Then, he put on his clothes. After he got dressed, he ate breakfast. Finally, he brushed his teeth.

Unit 6: Writing a Letter

p. 112

Dear Grandma should be circled in red. Yolanda should be circled in blue. Love should be circled in green.
March 3, 2005

p. 113

Victor
cans

p. 114

June 2, 2005 should be circled in red. Dear Mrs. Simms should be circled in blue. Thank you for being my teacher this year. You helped me so much. I loved learning the songs you taught us. My favorite song was the one about the speckled frogs. I will miss you next year. Have a great summer vacation! should be circled in green. Your student should be circled in yellow. Kelly should be circled in orange.

p. 116

Jamal wrote the letter.
He wrote it to his mom and dad.
They sat by a campfire and sang songs.

p. 117

September 12, 2005

Dear ashley,

¶ I hope you like your new house. I was very sad to see you move away, but I know you will make lots of friends at your new school. My mom says we can visit soon⊙ I can't wait! I will bring your favorite game. We can eat pizza and stay up all night, just like we used to do. I (*miss* mis) you very much. Please write ~~write~~ back soon!

Your friend,

Vonda

p. 119

Officer Brown
bike safety
Robert's dad

p. 120

november 12, 2005

Dear Aunt Rebecca,
(*Thank* Thnak) you so much for the pretty scarf⊙ it was such a nice birthday gift. Now that the weather is getting cooler here, I think I will wear it almost every day! each time I wear it, I will think of you and smile.

Love,

haley

p. 122

Sarah
A school carnival

p. 123

Invitation will vary but should include event, date, time, and place.

p. 125

Jake wrote the letter.
He wanted to tell Mr. Smith he is sorry for denting his car door.